zendoodle coloring

Winter Wonderland

Other great books in the series

zendoodle coloring

Baby Animals

Calming Swirls

Cozy Cats

Creative Sensations

Enchanting Gardens

Inspiring Zendalas

Into the Forest

Magical Fairies

Tranquil Gardens

Tropical Paradise

Under the Sea

Uplifting Inspirations

Winter Wonderland

Seasonal Delights to Color and Display

illustrations by

Jodi Best

ST. MARTIN'S GRIFFIN
NEW YORK

www.stmartins.com

ISBN 978-1-250-10880-7 (trade paperback)

Our books may be purchased in bulk for promotional, educational, or business use.
Please contact your local bookseller or the Macmillan Corporate and Premium
Sales Department at 1-800-221-7945, extension 5442, or by e-mail
at MacmillanSpecialMarkets@macmillan.com.

First Edition: October 2016

10 9 8 7 6 5 4 3 2 1

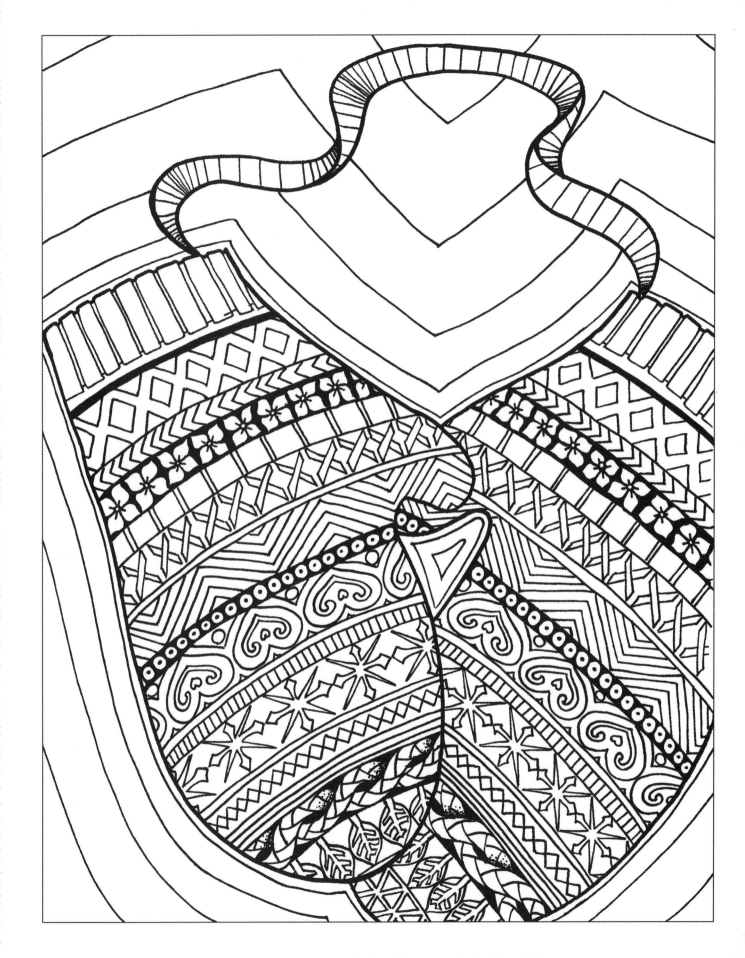

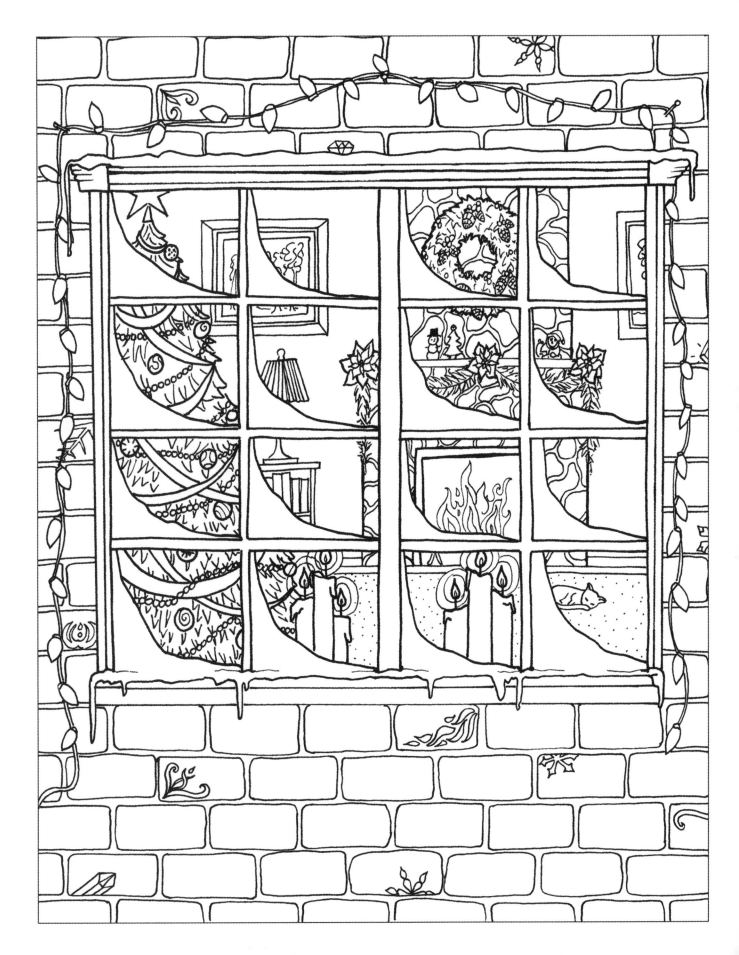